THE CHOCOLATE ROOM

Welcome to Dental,
Amanda!.

Paige Mead

THE CHOCOLATE ROOM

Exploring the Dental Industry as your next Professional Sales Career Destination

Paige Mead

JONES MEDIA PUBLISHING

To Lance, my perfect match

CONTENTS

Acknowledgements

FOR OPENING DOORS to me, I'm forever grateful to: Ken Skaught, Lori Isbell, Ivy Meadors, John Zimmer, Rob Mitchell, Jeff Denney, Rob Hays and Nathan Mead. Special thanks go to Gary Kirkus, CEO and to the authors of "History of Atlanta Dental Supply," Perry and David P. Blackshear (1970).

INTRODUCTION

THE DENTAL INDUSTRY has a rich and curious history. It's high tech and highly competitive, which is great for driving innovation. There's plenty of room to grow for a sales professional with talent and determination. Dental is a big-little place, a universe in a fishbowl. You can touch one segment of the industry, and from the right vantage point see the effects ripple across the whole thing. It's the perfect size to level-up your professional game and make an impact as an individual player.

The dental industry also has a "true" *multi-generational workforce*. Because we hear so much about different generations in the workforce these days, it's easy to conclude we really know what that walks and talks like.

In dental in the US, multigenerational workforce is a highly visible concept. As someone who enjoys sociology and anthropology, I'm a kid in a candy store. Even when I talk with veteran dental reps, it's not difficult to surprise them with new information about the industry they've spent their careers in. In truth, it's easy. All I have to say is "robotics" and minds are blown.

Before I give you the lay of the land, let's address why you should care. As a professional who wants to earn an impressive income in healthcare sales, why invest time on the backstory of the dental industry? You tell me: When you get married, will you care about your spouse's backstory? In the same way as dating matters to the beginning of a relationship, your research and due diligence on the industry you're considering is the prep-work you do when you care about where the relationship goes. Want to make an excellent match with your next sales role? Date well and thoroughly. With me here, now you're dating, prospecting. Interviewing is courting, and an offer of employment is a marriage proposal. Accepting that offer, verbally or in writing, is marriage. No joke. But here together, in this meager tome, we're dating the dental industry. And this is just a first date.

I have this exact conversation with different professional salespeople every day. It's subject matter all my sales candidates need to some degree and enjoy hearing about. While eye-opening, it isn't practical for me to have this conversation with one person at a time; it makes introductions to individual candidates the only work I can really get done. I love that part of my career, don't get me wrong, but sharing this vital information efficiently gives me more time for uncovering new sales opportunities I can then share with you.

You may be a sales professional in another healthcare industry who wants a different quality of life, but without having to sacrifice income or the professionalism of working with clinicians in a field that makes a substantial difference in people's lives. You may be a newbie to professional sales as a career and want to be in healthcare, but have never considered dental as a place in which to specialize. Alternately, you may be a talented sales professional who is already in the dental industry but had your nose to the grindstone, and, frankly, don't know what the heck is going on in the industry since the last time you looked for a role. You may even be a clinical professional who's been *wooed* by the idea of a sales career outside of the practice.

Whatever window you're looking at dentistry through, you're reading this book because someone has suggested to you it could be a great place to grow your sales career. This lay-of-the-land-conversation is for you. You're in the right place. Let's find out if the dental industry is a potential match for you and your sales career.

I've chosen to specialize my recruiting career in the dental industry because I find good chemistry with the relationships. To keep to the fishbowl analogy, there are several dynamic ecosystems. I began my recruiting career in the staffing industry over twenty years ago working with multiple industries and a global search firm. I tripped over dental in 2007, literally didn't see it coming.

When I say I love the sales profession in dental most, I'm not being cute. I've been able to look around and compare. I've run into some sharks here in dental, too. Yin and Yang. But, overall, the dental industry is still quite idyllic as healthcare spaces go. It's a place you can get passionate about, even fall in love with, and change lives significantly. It's common to hear things here like, "No one dies in the dental chair." It hardly sounds like the marketing message you'd expect to hear. "Well, at least no one dies over here..."

Yet, when it comes to quality of life in a healthcare sales career, it's extremely relevant. It's part of what makes the industry idyllic. Think of me as an ambassador from the dental industry, a resource for you as you consider your values in picking a new career home and employer. To hire on with a company is to get married to it. That bears repeating. To hire on with a company is to get married to it. Give your decision all the respect it deserves.

Heads up: if you're new to my backyard-universe-candy store-industry, considering dental as a career destination for the first time, you'll need a short list of terms to help you navigate discussions of employment and understand what you're getting into. I've included that list in the glossary just for you. Also, I mix metaphors.

Chapter 1

The Chocolate Room

I'LL BET THAT I've shared a version of this introduction to the dental industry with sales professionals more than 150 times over the last five years. That's a conservative estimate, but still an imaginable number. I came into this plucky industry through the distribution channel in 2007, and spent several learning years there before launching my firm in late 2014. When I think back over what I've learned about dental and business in the US since then, I wish I'd recorded some of those earlier versions of the story. In fact, I thought I had this conversation down rote when I started writing this book, and discovered otherwise.

For as fast as this industry grows and changes, a then-versus-now comparison might have made an interesting chapter to include here. It isn't possible to tell the same story of this industry in exactly the same way from one week to the next, let alone from one year to the next. The dental industry is a lot of things, but boring isn't one of them. A few weeks ago, I was trying to explain why I was writing this book to a friend who doesn't come from dental and isn't a sales professional, mostly to assure her I hadn't lost my mind. We were on a video call. To put my interest in the subject into context for her and give her a frame of reference, I started telling a story from the industry that I've told a number of times. It tasted stale in my mouth unexpectedly, falling short of what I was feeling at the time. She could see the confusion on my face, followed by a dawning awareness. "Wait. I'm realizing that this isn't the story I want to tell you." Seconds later, this came out...

"Remember that scene in *Willy Wonka and the Chocolate Factory* (original movie version with Gene Wilder) where Wonka shows his guests the garden where everything they see is made of candy? Like a childhood heaven, it has every different kind of confection you can imagine, but more to the point, every kind you *never* imagined: trees that grow ginormous candy canes and drop jaw-breakers all over the ground when Wonka walks by; flowers shaped like tea cups you drink honey from; beach balls with chocolate frosting inside them; a chocolate waterfall churning a chocolate river! Remember? A wonderland...and all of it you could put in your mouth! Voila! The dental industry."

Most of us have seen that movie at one point or another since it was made in 1971, and it's easy to recall that moment of awe, watching those kids and their parents get to run out into that candy land in every direction and eat anything they wanted. Wonka called it *The Chocolate Room.*

Before I first discovered dental as a significant career destination for sales professionals, I had only one friend I knew of who "worked in dental," if you don't count my dentist, and I gave the industry zero consideration as a recruiter. At first blush, it seemed like a weird place to choose to be, purposefully, since I'm not from any type of dental background, and definitely not something one easily speaks about at parties when asked, "What do you do?" Not *fun* parties, anyway, or if I'm trying to make friends.

But, I was totally and completely wrong and uninformed at that point. I often think to myself it is an invisible industry to most people. Right up to the point where you're standing in the middle of it and realize what you're seeing. The wondrous Chocolate Room is how I see it today. This is what the floor of every dental convention looks like to me now. We've got distribution companies, manufacturing companies, start-ups and giants in the industry, making everything a dental clinician needs to practice and dreaming up solutions to problems most people have. International companies looking to launch their US operations make some of the most fascinating hiring partners I currently have. I can't wait to see what comes next!

In my experience recruiting in healthcare, the dental industry offers sales professionals the best quality of life. That's right, quality of life is better here. Dentistry is highly technical and competitive, but less cutthroat. What do I mean by that? I mean I find more integrity in business here among dental sales professionals than I have in other healthcare spaces. We have no O-R to be on call for 24/7, and you can make a very healthy financial living here with far less blood loss.

The point is, less stress for sales professionals. Dental is actually a big place, as healthcare spaces go. When I hear "dentistry is a small world," I think, that's only true if you are combining all other medical spaces together as the comparison. We are conditioned to see medicine separately from dentistry, as though the mouth isn't a highly vital part of the human body. As a recruiter, I see where dental and medical cross paths, but also know the dental industry is uniquely its own, like a stand-alone story. In terms of medical specialties, it's not actually a small place. Unlike in other healthcare spaces which are built around doctors you usually only see when you're sick or something isn't functioning in the body as it should, in dental, the doors are open, and they stay open to everyone.

Innovations in treatment, technology, products and services are hidden in plain sight every time you walk into your dentist's office for a preventive check-up or procedure. But once you can identify what you're really seeing, dental becomes a wonderland.

Another thought to share on this is that among sales professionals in the dental world, I find more people who are truly passionate about what they are selling and the impact they're having on other humans. It's not difficult to get excited about giving a human back their smile. Teeth matter to everyone. Boom. Pretty vital industry.

Our dentists here in the US come from all over the world, and most of them come to the profession because an important person in their lives was a dentist who made a positive impact on them. Some of them are entrepreneurs and inventors, while others just love teeth and keeping them healthy. Some of them have natural business acumen, some do not; some are small business owners, some work for corporations; some even end up choosing a sales career in this industry! They're all pioneers to one degree or another.

Depending on where they come from and live across our nation, their buying habits reveal aspects of the company cultures they plant in their practices. When I use the word *culture* in a professional sense, I'm referring to values in providing products and services, in working relationships, as well as purchasing preferences. How we like to make our purchases is a component of company culture which we'll discuss in more detail in future chapters.

Attending dental conventions is my chance to come face to face with my industry clients and potential future candidates, and with the customers we all serve in the industry ultimately. While I don't ever recruit sales candidates from the convention floor, never-ever, I make it a point to stay up to date on the companies coming into our industry and the products and services my candidates may be selling in their next roles. I relish the opportunity to get my hands on the technology and, "play with the sharp thingies," to quote a dental student friend of mine. I have more friends in dentistry now than I ever imagined.

Conventions are real sensory experiences for me. I attend them so I can imagine standing in your shoes while we discuss a sales opportunity and the company who's hiring for it. I find out how the technology works and what makes one competitive product better than another. Conventions are where I go to see and evaluate the competitive landscape and to learn about how products are really being received in the market. I watch and I listen. I want to be able to communicate with you in context that helps you fully grasp the employment opportunity and as many of the variables around it as possible.

That's how it becomes real for <u>both</u> of us. My clients count on that level of awareness, whether they know it or not, when they hire me to tell their stories to their most desirable candidates. As a professional recruiter, telling their stories *well* is a huge part of what I do. I need the pros, the cons, and everything in between, and a lot of that I pick up at dental conventions. Bottom line, your next career opportunity is so much more than a bit of stiff language in a job description or the next step on your personal ladder. Your next career opportunity in the dental industry is also mine. We are, you and I, mutually invested in your success, and I take my investments very seriously.

When I stand back and consider all the players in the dental industry, something conventions allow for particularly well, I see that dental is a dynamic wonderland. From my perch in the US dental market, I can see the whole thing top-down and bottom-up. It's an incredible view.

CHAPTER 2

BACKYARDS & BACKSTORIES IN DENTAL

I CHOOSE NOT to be a W2'd employee and recruit for a single company because I need to play in multiple backyards. I want and *need* diverse hiring experiences. With my clients' successes in mind, independence in my career affords me that ability along with regular opportunities to test out and upgrade my skills. If I was a full-time recruiter, W2'd for just one company, it would be like standing in Wonka's Chocolate Room and only eating one thing, over and over and over. I'd get bored, and my perspective would shrivel. I don't know about you, but for me, boredom is a fate worse than death.

As an independent contractor, my experiences in multiple company environments are cumulative and ever-expanding. Every single backyard is different in highly educational ways, and most offer pleasant surprises just about every time I visit. The backyards that aren't friendly or pleasant also contain big lessons, just the kind you only want to visit once. They are few and far between in the dental industry, fortunately. In five years of business, and roughly fifty clients so far, I've only discovered four I won't play with or in again.

There's a company in the dental industry that was founded in part through the early networking efforts of one John Henry Holliday, DDS, aka *Doc Holliday*. Friends with Wyatt Earp? Shootout at the OK Corral ringing any bells? If you've never heard the name *Doc Holliday*, there's a great article in the journal, *Chairside Magazine: Volume 7, Issue 2*, which sums up *Doc's* story nicely. Or you can just watch the movie *Tombstone* and hold the facts loosely. I recommend partaking of both, actually. My point is the trade side of the dental industry has some fun facts. The real *Doc Holliday* practiced dentistry in Georgia, where he introduced his cousin, Dr. Robert Holliday, DDS to a colleague, Dr. Samuel C. Hape just after the Civil War. Robert Holliday started the Pennsylvania College of Dental Surgery in 1856, where *Doc* graduated with his dental degree. Samuel Hape owned a dental supply company in Atlanta where *Doc* would first set up his practice.

Post-Civil War, Hape sold the company to Dr. Robert Holliday, and its name was changed to Atlanta Dental Supply. This pioneering company is still alive and kicking today in 2020, growing, expanding, and profitable. Side note: tuberculosis inspired our *Doc Holliday* to move *out* West and practice dentistry where the climate was drier. Coughing fits would eventually scare away his patients, at which point he did what any professional clinician in his situation would do: he began a life of gambling and gun-slinging. But I digress.

Privately held and employee-owned, Atlanta Dental Supply's expert salesforce now offers clinicians an array of technology for the practice that would've boggled the minds of Hape and Holliday and excited them for the future of dentistry. This backstory isn't alone among those that can be told of US-born dental companies, over 100 years old and aging well. The late 1800s were significant times for dental distribution companies to come alive in the US, and for dental schools to open their doors for the first time as well.

Distribution companies enabled the practice of dentistry to travel from east coast to west coast and blossom all along the way. Dental distributors fueled the growth of dentistry as a US industry. These companies who brought clinicians a more consistent stream of tools and supplies also offered variety in materials and equipment for the first time. They brought choices in products and services that freed the dentist to do what they loved to do, practice dentistry.

Independent dental distributors were responsible in part for spreading advancements in dental education and innovations in practice. They were visionaries. Companies like Atlanta Dental Supply, and Burkhart Dental Supply, on the west coast, brought professionalism and sophistication to the practice of dentistry. A more local place to go for supplies meant a dentist could spend time seeing patients, and more of them, instead of traveling; they could literally *practice* dentistry. Dig into the history of dental distribution in the US to begin to understand the private practice dentist and how this client is wired. Unlike in dental manufacturing, the owners and families that spawned the distribution companies in dental are the most alike our private practice dentists. Just like our doctors, they're small business owners, often engineering-minded, rebellious, artists, and students, and many were clinicians themselves.

The independent dental distributor truly has the private practice dentist's best interests in mind, because they are living the battle of whether or not to consolidate, side-by-side, elbow-to-elbow with the independent dentist. They see eye-to-eye. I'm sure other company leaders do too, but not like the owners of the independent distribution companies. It's just a phenomenon you have to experience. The future pathway for dental distribution is shaped like a question mark at the moment. The consolidation of companies selling to our doctors, not to mention the consolidation *of* our doctors and their practices, might strike fear in many hearts, but not mine. Industry consolidation isn't the death knoll of anything. It's the sign of industry evolution. I'm not saying that company consolidation is something to work toward, necessarily. Independence has a nice ring to it. I'm a fan. I'm saying it's inevitable, as product delivery systems go, for companies to come together and change—and necessary in order to make room for the metamorphosis of buying habits that's taking place among this latest generation of dentists who are graduating into the US workforce. They've grown up on the internet!

Today's graduating clinicians are used to doing their own research on products and services, or at the very least, reading reviews about what other people who've done their own research have to say about products and services. The sharpest distributors have that in mind and plan for it. I have tremendous respect for the distributors in the dental industry, and they're in an evolutionary process. Independence is still a battle cry and a virtue highly valued in this industry. But size also matters to a company's ability to provide the best products and services to price-conscious buyers. I'm not of the opinion that distribution is dead, or even dying. *How* our clients get the products and services they need to run their practices continues to be crucial to independence itself. This is one of the reasons I enjoy looking at the history of distributors here because it's an entire picture that correlates directly with the changes we've seen over time, and are seeing now, in how our doctors choose to practice and purchase the tools of their trade.

Choice is the key. If you like options, and a lot of them, then distribution is definitely not "dead." Choice and independence go hand in hand, particularly in dentistry. I would even go so far as to say that if a dentist wants to continue to have choices in how they practice, independently or as part of a corporation, for example, they should elect to buy from independent dental distributors whenever possible. Now there's a spicy dinner conversation topic for you. If you don't end up selling professionally for a distribution company, at least understand their role in the origins of the industry in the US. If you neglect to, you'll always only have a fractional understanding of the industry. You can get along without the full picture, but it's short-sighted, and really, why would you want to?

Now that I've made such a big deal about the distribution side of dental, let's talk manufacturing, the companies that make the tools of the trade for dentistry, and incidentally, make up most of my client base. I wouldn't be here without them. If distribution is the zoo, manufacturing makes up all the animals in the zoo. For me, going to a dental convention is a trip to the zoo as much as it is to the Chocolate Room. Some dental manufacturers can seem more outwardly interesting, flashy, even, while others become increasingly interesting as you investigate them. The sheer variety of manufacturers in the dental industry, let alone their products, provides a zoo too large to visit in a single day.

By the same token, looking at the dental industry from the angle of a professional sales career destination, you have a plethora of choices in how you sell, what you sell, whom you sell for, and whom you sell to. Side note: I never thought I would geek-out over dentistry; I'm a very anxious dental patient, I confess. But I did learn recently, that if my dentist just talks with me about what technology he's thinking about purchasing for his practice this year, my mind is back at the zoo. It works like a charm. I wish I'd figured that out years ago, but better late than never for my oral health's sake.

In order to understand my clients best, and really get to know them, I visit their company headquarters as soon in my relationship with them as possible. I need this visit to their backyards as part of experiencing their company culture. At any given time, I try to work with at least one manufacturer in every product segment in the industry so my viewpoint is well-rounded, including multiple backyards for perspective and insight. I learn more about my industry by working within different environments and teams, and I choose my clients, in part, based on the lessons I can learn while working with them.

Choice and variety with dental manufacturing clients are important to my independence as well. I specialize in the dental industry for all of the reasons I advocate joining the industry as a sales professional. It's the Chocolate Room; the universe in a fishbowl; an outstanding community with a lot of cool backyards to explore and learn in: supplies/merchandise, core equipment, digital technology, practice management software, lab-side products and services, sleep dentistry, dental implants (med device), and yes, robotics. And these are just the backyards I've explored to date!

One innovation begets the next, and start-ups are coming into the industry at a rapid pace. When it comes to all the choices in products and employers you have as a sales professional in dental, take my advice: explore, explore, explore before you choose. Do your research. Know the backstory. Date thoroughly. Understand the influences that helped develop the product itself, as well as those that will shape its reception in the market and its future relevance to the profession. When you think dynamically about the industry, as a sales professional, you're better equipped to assist your customers in making strong purchasing decisions for their practices. That's when you become a true consultant and business partner.

Chapter 3

What Type of Sales Rep Are You?

I LIKE WORKING with start-ups a lot, and I love the fact dental is an industry where you find inventors, risk-takers, and disruptors. They make fun dates, and they keep the industry exciting; but they aren't everyone's marriage partners.

I love the oldies but goodies, too, as far as clients go. These are the manufacturers who make the staples every practicing dentist needs and buys, and won't do without. As a recruiter, I want them both as clients, and I can have them both because I maintain my independence. You can have both too if you carry an independent sales bag and decide to represent multiple products and manufacturers at one time.

An independent sales professional has those options. But if the idea of being an independent isn't for you, if you want to be a W2'd sales professional, playing on one team in one backyard, then you need to know what type of sales rep you naturally are and what environment you need to sell in to be most successful in whatever way you define career success. Know the way you sell best in order to pick the best marriage partner for your sales career.

If you need a refresher on types of sales and types of sales reps, now would be a good time to jump to the back and read the crib notes. I've outlined a number of types of sales professional profiles so you have points of reference for identifying your style and nature for selling. You are more likely to be one type or another versus to choose one type or another. But don't be naive or uninformed—figure it out. "Knowledge is power," to quote my favorite *Schoolhouse Rock* jingle. Side-note: yes, dear reader, I am aware that "knowledge is power," as a direct quote can be attributed to early

Persian writers dating as far back as pre-Christ. But I assure you, this reference is much more fun to sing.

Hunters. As a sales professional, are you a hunter? If you are, the hunt is your source of energy and build-up to the win. It's fast-paced and constant. You need stamina for the hunt. Account managers, by contrast, are energized when they are managing and caring for their clients and doing more of the hand-holding. These two don't have to be mutually exclusive in a professional sales role, however, and in fact, many roles require a combination of regular hunting and hand-holding. But the fact remains that without the hunt, the hunter will lose interest in the game, and without the hand-holding, the account manager will lose interest in the game.

Mismatched, both outcomes result in a loss. If you fail to take this into account when you are in pursuit of your next sales role, you'll be setting yourself up for work that feels like work, rewards you like work, and drains your energy like work. In other words, your sales role will feel like a counter-productive grind. I like failure as a teaching tool, but it hurts an awful lot when your job is on the line, which is exactly where it will be if you toss this wisdom to the wayside.

Are you both hunter and account manager? To what degree are you more of one than the other? What happens to your motivation once you've hunted so successfully your territory has grown too large for anything but account management? What happens to your motivation when you're in a scratch territory but you're really wired for account management? Are you a W2 or a 1099? Are you a manufacturer rep or a distributor rep? Brand-loyal or brand-disruptive? What happens to you once your disruptive brand becomes standard of care? What does *standard of care* even mean as it relates to your natural sales aptitude?

Did you know so many questions would be up in the air when you decided to embark on a professional sales career? You need to be able to answer the questions honestly and patch together the picture of who you are and what you do best to be the most powerful version of you. It's not always simple to figure out, especially when the best teacher is most often experience. I honestly love her, but she can be a *real b----*.

As a sales professional, though, you knew this job was dangerous when you took it. This career is not for the faint of heart. If you know professional sales is the career for you, great, you're halfway there. Deciding how, what, and for whom to sell are processes of elimination when you have all the variables in front of you.

In terms of how you're wired as a sales professional, territories may require a combination of both hunting and account management, but rarely is one individual a true blend of both roles and personality types, 50/50. You will naturally incline toward one or the other, and utilizing the opposite skill set is a *sometimes* thing, kind of like eating cake. If you set yourself up in a sales role that requires you to spend more of your time, or most of your time, utilizing the selling skill that isn't your natural state, you will live in stress and discomfort. That's a fact. You will hate your job, and your motivation and energy will flag and die in flames. You will have limited success at best if you choose the wrong selling environment or product for yourself. When you truly need to find a job, the decisions won't feel very clean-cut and easy. Sometimes, we just need to work. As a part of being human, work is good for us. But if you have the time to choose critically, please, please, dear reader, don't let your desire to be employed override your knowledge of what constitutes a successful selling role with an employer who is well-matched for you. To do so is to wed with divorce in mind. Ouch.

Take the decision to sell for a distributor versus a manufacturer. As lessons in selling go, this is an important one because jumping from manufacturing to distribution, or vice versa, is really difficult once you start down a path in the dental industry, or any healthcare sale, for that matter. It's not impossible, but it usually takes a year or more to find the right entry point, and both sides are not in a hurry to alienate a partner in business by hiring from them. Manufacturers and distributors need each other. Hiring and firing are expensive for everyone involved. In short, it's complicated to make the leap in either direction. A sales professional who thrives in distribution is not the same as one who thrives in manufacturing—how you sell a product or service is markedly different in these two environments.

I remember noting in my first years in dental the trend was for reps to move toward a distribution role, as they were highly coveted. I maintain launching a dental distribution territory from scratch is the most difficult selling role in the industry. As opinions go, I'm sure that one won't win me many fans on the manufacturing side, but it's based in data on turnover and time-to-profit among distributors across the dental industry that I've been measuring since 2007. This role deserves its place among highly coveted positions. But today, as distributors work to accommodate the way dentists like to buy products— on the internet—the trend is reversed and more reps are asking about manufacturing opportunities.

There are definitely products that lend themselves best to those who are wired to be account managers and who may enjoy a sales career in distribution: we call them consumables, or supplies, and that category of product renews its value as a sale on a regular and predictable basis. In distribution, the products being sold are to a large degree consumable, and clients need them week after week, month after month. Every rep likes to have consumables in the bag. The client with a consumable, or renewable need, requires account management because the needs are so constant, and also because, due to the consistency of reps visiting the practice, consumable sales tend to be most easily lost. Thus, the hand-holding and frequent visits.

By contrast, a product your clinician may only purchase once in a while, perhaps yearly or once every few years, requires a sales professional who is wired to be a hunter, and not only that. This hunter needs to enjoy a longer sales cycle. Finding the brand new buyer is what brings a hunter renewed energy and motivation, short sales cycle or long.

While there are definitely products sold by dental distributors that fit this category, most hunter-focused products and services are found on the manufacturing side of the house. Manufacturing tends to be the preferred destination of reps who want to sell a smaller bag of products in order to specialize, or who don't enjoy the hand-holding that comes with account management. You can, however, find account management-oriented selling roles at both manufacturers and distributors, consumables in both arenas, and hunting is a skill no successful sales professional ever totally sets down.

The dental industry is varied enough to have many options on both sides of the house, and clinicians have regular needs for both. As far as clients go, dentists are good like that. Still, the distribution rep sees the fullest possible picture of the business their clinicians run. They're also the ones who tend to get the closest to their customer because they see them more often than other reps do. This sales professional is ideally a consultative partner to the dentist, and one trained to understand how the business of dentistry actually works. To date, most dental schools don't teach future clinicians how to run successful businesses. To a clinician who desperately needs this training, or who would prefer to practice dentistry rather than run the business, the distribution rep can be a lifesaver, or business-saver, as the case may be. The distribution rep has the car that all the manufacturing reps who sell through distribution want to ride in.

The exception to this is the manufacturing rep who sells direct to the dentist. Sans-distributor rep has become a popular way to sell in recent years, as many manufacturing reps I talk with prefer not to have to work through other sales reps to get their products into the dentist's hands.

The phrase *herding cats* comes to mind. The manufacturing rep also needs to be selling consultatively and tends to be more hunter-focused on the whole. Any successful sales professional always hunts for new business. (Please read that last sentence twice.) But as a distribution territory grows, account management becomes a more focal need and there is simply less time for hunting and cold-calling. If you don't prefer the hand-holding involved in account management to the pace of hunting, you may want to aim for a manufacturing role that sells direct to the dentist.

Manufacturers sell either through distribution, direct, or both. If you want to see your clinicians more often, and truly enjoy the hand-holding, distribution may be ideal for you. Or you may want to select an employer that manufactures consumables primarily. When you sell as a distributor, you are the specialist who offers choices. When you sell as a manufacturer, you are the specialist on your product. Smaller bag, tighter specialization, but fewer choices. You'd better believe in your company and product offering whole-heartedly if you hire on with a dental manufacturer. The time you spend analyzing what type of sales professional you naturally are, and which kind of selling you're drawn to will be well worth it. Remember, once you hire on, it's difficult to switch sides.

Emerging technologies, start-ups, and restart-ups are launching all over the dental industry and bringing change with them that could just as easily be a flash in the pan as alter the dental industry permanently. Not every product you come across in your investigation of the industry has staying power. Not every new technology will present a viable value proposition.

Some products do and will, but the company who first brings them to market might fail for lack of a sustainable company culture or inadequate funding. Company culture is fluid in the early stages of a start-up, which adds to the risk inherent in working for one. Start-ups are generally disruptive to existing methods, practices, and ideals, and it takes a certain type of risk-loving, highly adaptable person to sell in a start-up environment and challenge status-quo, particularly in dental.

But that's what being part of a start-up is all about. It's big risk, high stakes, and no manual. Sometimes I have the good fortune of working with a sales candidate who knows they want a strong, well-known brand to represent, and a product that isn't going out of style any time soon. A sales rep who knows they thrive in disruptive environments with products few have heard of or seen before is also fun to work with. These are clear preferences articulated by experienced sales reps who know how they work best. The point isn't which side of the spectrum they land on, it's that they know themselves that makes a successful job search possible. You're either well-suited to sell in a start-up environment or you're not. It isn't something you learn to be, and most people are not well-suited to usher in disruption. For those of you who are avidly seeking the thrill of a start-up experience, here are three things to keep in mind while you watch for the opportunities:

1. **Expect chaos.** No matter what. Chaos in the job description, in the role itself, and in every nook and cranny of the start-up organization. I can't emphasize this enough: if you're looking to work for a start-up that's well-organized and behaves like a mature company, you aren't ready for any start-ups. Chaos is the name of the game in the beginning years of every start-up. It's not a sign of a poorly baked idea, nor of a sketchy leadership team. Building something from nothing only works flawlessly if you're God.

2. **Company culture is fluid** in the beginning. Think of a start-up as a brand-new baby, human or animal. They throw up on you, cry, poop, and make you feel amazing— sometimes all at once. The same goes for a start-up. Sleepless nights and long days with your new infant company will feel like a marathon with no end in sight. Your baby company won't take on a solid cultural framework for at least three years because every process, application, and role is new. You'll be able to see the company take shape over time, but change in the early years is such a constant that to measure a company's culture while it's in start-up mode is akin to predicting adult features at the time of birth: you'll have informed guesses, but nothing's guaranteed.

If you haven't had the pleasure of parenting, human or animal, you can also think of it like baking a cake. The beginning of the process looks nothing like the end, especially when you've done it right. It's a mixture made up of multiple ingredients in a state of chemical change right up until it's fully baked. Forget a crucial aspect of the process, and your cake falls flat. Like building a company from scratch, it's a delicate process which you affect with the addition of each ingredient. But you won't know specifically what you've created until it's fully baked and cooled.

3. **Commitment equals 150%.** Plan to invest yourself in raising the baby, or the cake, and know that there is no such thing as "work-life balance" in a start-up. You *will* work harder, longer hours, and with less pay in the early years. That's normal, and to be expected. Kiss your vacations goodbye, at least for the first few years of the company's life, and expect the infant creation to take over your world.

These lessons are absolute in a start-up company regardless of the role you're in and the work you're accountable for. If this scares you away from start-ups, good. Just like having a baby, no one is ever truly ready. But if you're expecting the poop and the barf, you'll also be there for the joy. It's just going to be a long haul. Count on it.

Questions to ask yourself:

Do you prefer a shorter sales cycle or a longer one?

Do you want to spend your time hand-holding or prospecting?

Do you enjoy "windshield time," or flights, and how often?

Do you want to be home in your own bed most nights, or are you a road warrior?

Do you like to sell products at the best price or the premium products?

Do you like to sell products that no one has ever heard of before and buck the system? Or do you prefer to sell with a strong brand?

Larger salary and smaller commission, or lower salary and uncapped commission potential?

Stable and somewhat predictable or start-up? Risky or less risky?

Presumably, you've decided on a sales career, and no sales career is completely without risk. But there are definitely degrees of risk to consider.

If you're an experienced sales professional, more than likely you've figured out the answers to some of these questions along the path of your career. But if you are new to professional sales, you may not even have known the questions existed. Your ability to identify which type of sales professional you are, the products and services you will be most successful selling, and the type of client relationships you want will aid you in finding the professional sales role that matches you. Point being, your career match will take time and effort to identify. Furthermore, time and life will change you, and your preferences for how and what you like to sell will change with you.

As with the choice between manufacturing and distribution, it's crucial to understand your nature on these topics as well, and to pay attention as time passes. Figure out what type of sales pro you are, how you sell the best, as well as what products and services and sales cycles are in your sweet spot, because your selling success depends in large part on fully comprehending the choices and choosing well.

I hope it's starting to become really clear why it's important to understand as much about your industry and yourself as you possibly can. Here, it's about knowing dental *and* being able to pinpoint exactly where you can step into it for maximum success in your career.

CHAPTER 4

THE SECRET TO CULTURE FIT

WHEN MY DENTAL sales candidates know their finish lines, their starting lines, and their values, career discussions are very promising. I've known for a long time I enjoy helping sales professionals get where they want to go in their careers. That's the coach/ cheerleader in me. But knowing the destination is of primary importance in the sales career discussion.

When I speak with a new sales candidate, our conversation always begins in the same way: "Where do you want your career to go?" The reason it's the first question I ask is that if the person I'm talking with doesn't have a clue where they want to end up, there's not much I can do to help them get there. On the other hand, if you can envision a finish line for your career, then at least I can help you aim. If you're reading this and unsure of your career destination, you're not alone. I wish it was less common ground than it is, but there are more sales professionals who don't know where they want to be when they wrap up their careers than those who do.

When I first launched my business, I was routinely surprised by this. But I've found sales pros at all stages of their careers who couldn't tell me where they were heading. In cases where the sales candidate is over the age of forty, let's say, it's possible to attribute some of the confusion to the fact that as generations move through the workforce, how we think about and relate to work changes along with it. In the dental industry more than any other industry I've worked in, industry veterans making job changes frequently have been with one employer since they graduated from school and weren't planning on needing to make a change. With this age group particularly, it used to be that you went to work because work was *good for you*, and everyone needed to work. The only hard part was finding a job versus the job.

Employment didn't change with passions the way it does in today's economy. So, it isn't uncommon at all for me to speak with someone heading into their second career in dental who needs to identify a new finish line. When they come to that level of awareness in conversation with me, it's often with a little remorse. Fortunately, learning about the choices we all have can be very rejuvenating. Where we want to go in our careers is typically the part we all secretly know in our hearts, but perhaps feel sheepish about expressing out loud, even to ourselves.

For example, with a little prodding, a candidate might think for a moment, and then say with surprising confidence, "I want to finish my career with enough money in the bank to allow me to pay the bills and travel the world." Or a candidate may say, "I want to be the CEO or GM of a company." Both are equally fabulous examples of *where* they want to go with their career. Once that first where is excavated from the caverns of the heart, the conversation usually takes on more energy and enjoyment.

Think about it now. Where do you want to end up in your sales career? Are you a career sales rep, a hunter, or account manager who finds ultimate satisfaction in cultivating a growing sales territory? Maybe you envision yourself leading a sales organization for a company as a director or VP of sales. Maybe you've gone to the top levels in a company, and have learned along the way you prefer to be right there with your team in the trenches. Maybe you're a rookie sales rep and *think* you know where you want your finish line to be. But you won't *actually* know until you're running for a while. Life will shake you up at times.

The point isn't that your finish line never changes along the way, but that you have one to begin with. Can you be in a professional sales career without having a finish line in mind? Yep, of course, and many people do. But if you get laid off or terminated, or life throws you some other curveball you weren't expecting, it will be harder than it needs to be to course-correct without a point of reference. Where is your career finish line?

Identifying your starting line comes next. The first *where* is a decision; the second *where* is a matter of fact. The reason identifying your starting line comes after identifying your finish line is because the two are relative. You won't be able to know where you are until you have the context of where you want to go. From your starting line, you can plot your course, determine what skills and experience you have vs what you need to keep running toward your goal, and set about designing a plan to get to the finish line you have in mind for your sales career.

If you know professional sales is for you, and you know what type of selling is in your nature, even those two things constitute a starting line. If your finish line is a sales management role in the dental industry and you haven't yet begun your first professional B2B sales role, or if you don't know what B2B is, then you've identified your starting line, and dragging down your first B2B role is step one on your way to your finish line. If you are already in your first B2B role, then you're at your starting line and you may need to find your first healthcare sales role as a step toward your finish line.

B2B selling is necessary for any successful professional sales career in healthcare, including the dental industry. With both the finish line and starting line determined, where you want to go in your career, and where you are beginning from, plotting the course between the two becomes possible. I enjoy that conversation with my candidates, but I couldn't have it very effectively without knowing my industry and how to navigate it, or without the candidate knowing their starting and finishing lines.

Your *why* in this career discussion is about your values. Your values are a guardrail with respect to choosing what type of company culture you work in to get to your career finish line. Your values shape the reasons for the choices you make. To identify the company culture you will thrive in professionally, you need to know concretely what you value in life and find a company who shares your values. It doesn't matter how effectively you've plotted the course of your career, if you fail to identify employers who share your values, the way will be longer and more arduous than it needs to be because you won't feel like part of the team at work.

Without shared values, the sales professional and their company will find at some point their destinations don't match either, and they will part ways. Aligning with your employer in culture, in values, is just one part of a great employment experience, but it's a huge part. We refer to this state of aligned values as culture fit. How do I figure out what the company-slash-employer values? Answer: look at their buying decisions as a company for clues.

Consider the difference between a person who buys frugally and values saving money when making purchases, and a person who buys only the premier options on a regular basis, valuing quality over cost savings. Those two people will see the buying decision profoundly differently and aren't likely to work together well at all. If a company makes buying decisions valuing frugality, that can look "cheap" to a sales rep working for them who values quality over low price and equates quality with premium brands. The frugal company will frequently disappoint the brand-loyal sales rep, and neither the company nor the rep will find a match for a long-term relationship.

How we make purchasing decisions is an indicator of our values, and values predict company culture. In case another example is helpful, consider the difference between a company who believes the customer is always right, and the sales rep who may not agree. If the company needs to choose a side when a customer has an issue, and believes the customer is always right, the sales rep may feel "sacrificed" by the company and want to leave them. The company will appear to prefer losing their rep over their customer. That smarts like a betrayal when you've been a loyal employee. Is it any wonder so many people hurt so deeply when they lose their employment? It isn't just a matter of money and lost wages. Losing your employment is a tangible and emotional loss that takes a tangible and emotional toll. If lacking culture fit leads inevitably to separation, why would anyone take a job or hire a person without it? Right. Even when it's amicable, the separation is costly for both sides, emotionally and financially. It's a big 'effing mess regardless of which side you're on.

The ownership level of a company sets its culture. Culture doesn't change unless something about the company's foundational structure changes—for example, when ownership changes hands during a merger or acquisition. Let's consider briefly what it looks like when two companies attempt a merger without culture fit. Every time two companies attempt a merger, the original entities set aside their individuality to make it happen, and both companies' cultures get rocked to the core. Even in the best of circumstances, blending two previously separate corporate entities results in duplicated resources, chaos, and the collision of values. Just as if two humans were blended to become one, extra arms and organs would have to be managed. Which heart or brain do we keep? Which sales team is retained? Hopefully, the proper amount of dating took place between the two companies before they married and merged, because that's the only way to mitigate the mash-up.

To make it work, a whole new company culture has to be birthed from the ashes. The new company is a *restart-up*. As a present-day example of a restart-up, let's consider the cultural mash-up that occurred when Zimmer purchased its competitor, Biomet 3i, in 2014. Two tremendous companies in healthcare came together across verticals. I'm going to keep this example really high-level and focused in dental, but in the right atmosphere to evaluate culture fit between the two companies.

For a while, it was just painful to hear from sales professionals in the industry who were on either side of the mash-up experiencing value conflicts where their money and client loyalties were concerned. Reps and sales managers from both camps felt extreme discomfort and stress trying to blend compensation philosophies and ideal clients. Both companies sold their dental implant line to specialists in dentistry who traditionally placed them. But one of the companies, Zimmer, also sold the implants to general practitioners who traditionally did not place dental implants but were learning to add the discipline to their patient offerings.

For the Biomet team and clients, this required accepting a significant philosophical change that ran contrary to the idea of specialization. There wasn't a "bad guy" or a "villain" on either side, although it may have felt like it. They were two very different corporate cultures, both a fit for their individual sales organizations separately. Together, the two cultures didn't feel like a *fit* for either sales organization, and both sides experienced losses in terms of employee and client turnover along the way. It was very messy until the new culture started to emerge. I'd like to congratulate the folks who stuck it out in both camps, uniting under the vision of what was to come.

The point to take away here is this: sometimes the baby is ugly for a while whenever two company cultures become one. That's an event that breaks culture down and forces the collective organization to start over, rebuilding culture from the ground up and with consideration for mutual values. The good news for the baby is eye color eventually resolves, the brain and body parts learn to work together, and spontaneous barfing ceases, though it may take a handful of years to get there. But during early infancy, culture is fluid and incredibly fragile, and that goes for start-ups and restart-ups alike.

Identifying values and compatible culture is critical to making a successful match for companies and candidates alike. To that end, here are the three questions I use at the start of every new candidate introduction call I have:

1. Where's your career finish line? Where do you want to go?

2. Where is your starting line? Where are you now, and what steps have you taken to start tracking toward your finish line?

3. What do you value? This is the secret to culture fit with your employer.

Chapter 5

Choosing Your Next Move

WHEN YOU STEP into your next interview process, you will be able to evaluate the company as a potential employer and marriage partner by assessing company ownership structure, culture, turnover, and growth opportunities. In short, because you will have done your due diligence beginning with your own career goals and values, you'll be prepared to interview critically. I'm going to give you context for this assessment along with some key interview questions that will help you acquire the information you need.

Ownership Structure and Culture. Let's begin with who owns the company and pays the bills. How many owners are there? Is the owner active in the day-to-day business operations? Or has ownership hired a team to manage the business itself? The important factors to identify here have to do with where the owner's values are placed and where the financial interests lie objectively. Ownership, regardless of the form it takes, sets company culture. It isn't a matter of right or wrong in any case. It's a matter of knowing where the buck literally stops and what values drive the company itself, both financially and in community with the rest of the industry. Family-owned, employee-owned, venture-backed, publicly traded, the owner's values, or owners' values, will be the company's values overall.

With the internet at our fingertips, you can learn these details as long as the company is publicly traded. If it's a privately-held company, it isn't quite as easy, but still possible if you're resourceful. The owner's values prevail, and you can ask for evidence of them in your next interview. Once you know whose values drive the company, and what they are, identify how many leadership levels exist between owner and field execution team. Each leadership level adds a filter between the owner and sales professionals in the field who sell the company's products and services.

Essentially, the fewer the number of levels between owner and field team, the clearer the view on company culture. In evaluating a potential employer, follow the leadership down to the field level to see how the company's core values play out in the market. What are you looking for? First and foremost, for evidence ownership will walk their talk, and that the field team is in lockstep. So what does that look like? If the field team isn't in sync with ownership, the evidence will be excessive turnover in the sales organization, and among clients. The more levels of leadership you need to analyze, the more carefully you should investigate.

A larger company typically has more levels of leadership to examine, and if each layer is in harmony with the next, it will have a very strong corporate culture. An organization with a strong culture accompanied by consistency in business practices typically continues to grow in both profit and size. That's not to say a smaller company can't be highly profitable, have a strong culture, or choose to remain small. I find turnover in employees and client base goes hand in hand with a company whose culture isn't consistent throughout the organization, large or small, private or public.

The benefits of consistent company culture, when it comes to evaluating your potential experience with them as an employee, are that you will know whom you work for, and you will have a clear picture of character and values to hold up to your own for a match. In your next interview, ask your interviewer, *"What values would you say are most important for me, as a potential new sales rep and contributor, to share with the company's owners and leadership? Will you give me some examples of the company's values in action?"* I like these questions because they rarely produce a scripted response. More than likely, your interviewer will have to take a moment to think about their answers before providing you with their personal observations. You'll gain insight into the company as well as on your interviewer.

Growth Opportunities and Turnover. As a professional sales rep, the number of leadership levels in a company can tell you about the potential for upward mobility as well. The fewer the leadership levels, the smaller the company, and the higher the likelihood that someone above you in the company structure will have to die, retire, or get fired in order for you to move up in your career. If moving up the career ladder is important to you, multiple levels of leadership in an organization can be desirable. The larger the company, the more levels, the higher the likelihood that in order to advance in your career, no one directly above you in the chain has to die, retire, or be fired.

In a smaller organization with fewer leadership levels, there are fewer ways to grow professionally in the organization. A smaller company has a couple of choices when it comes to maintaining its structure and size: it can hire people who don't grow and keep a consistent workforce; or it can hire people with great career potential and experience turnover when and if there is nowhere for those people to grow within the organization. If you're the owner in a smaller company, you always get to be at the top. But if you're a growth-oriented sales professional in that same smaller company, you will have to make some tough decisions.

Maximizing your career growth may require you work for more than one company over the course of your career. We used to work in one company for as long as we could, and experience was determined with an eye to length of time in the role. But longevity at a company, or in one role, isn't as prevalent a value today in a marketplace where technology advances moment by moment. Remember what I said about multiple backyards. More and more it seems experience is measured with an eye to variety. Does that mean if you want to attain the level of CEO in a company you shouldn't choose to work for a small company? Not remotely. As educators in business, smaller companies can be amazing teachers! It means as a growth-minded sales professional you need to evaluate your potential employers for the lessons you'll learn while you're with them in addition to what you can bring them and contribute.

Smaller companies need to get more done with a lower headcount, meaning employees' plates can be very full. Compared to a large, matrixed organization, where roles and responsibilities are more clearly defined, (and exclusive), you can't beat a smaller company when it comes to the availability of comprehensive learning opportunities. You just may need to plan for your own turnover.

Changing employers no longer necessarily signals a lack of commitment on the employee's or employer's part. Now, movement in a person's career is just as likely to correspond to professional growth as to any less agreeable reason. When I see a resume with multiple job changes, I don't assume that I'm looking at a job-hopper. I consider the possibility that there may be risky start-ups involved, which as we've already discussed, make employment inconsistencies highly probable.

Reductions in workforce affect great sales people too. I was having a hiring conversation recently about turnover with a colleague who still believes *no good sales rep gets laid off*. At first, I was shocked he was still thinking that way when it occurred to me he hadn't been in the job market in more than 18 years and his intel had expired. Once upon a time, you only lost your job if you were bad at it, or did something really wrong. Being downsized as a sales professional in today's market may have little to do with being good at your job, and more likely be a cost-saving measure for a company whose budget is stretched too thinly. Lay-offs are common during mergers and acquisitions, as well as business divestitures. No company's workforce is totally immune anymore.

When I hear from veteran sales reps who've been in one role for the entirety of their career to-date and find themselves separated from that employment unexpectedly, as with a lay-off, they're often bewildered by the job market and uncertain how to go about finding another role. The landscape of the job market has changed dramatically in recent years. To add insult to injury, skills gained in only one type of selling environment get dull over time. Where once career longevity was highly regarded, today it can be construed as lacking experience in an evolving buyer's marketplace. Yikes! For those of you reading this who've experienced this very thing, it can feel like you've been sucker-punched. The last time you checked, it was *good* to be loyal to one employer, wasn't it? Isn't it still? Truly, we're in a market of significant generational overlap, value mash-ups, and unpredictability.

If you're reading this and considering a career move but haven't yet let go of existing employment, intentionally or otherwise, that's great news! You have the opportunity to evaluate the market against your own skills and upgrade before moving out. That's the plan I most highly recommend. Remain competitive. This is your goal, so when you are looking at your next company or career move, regardless of the other variables, you have sharpened skills to hunt with and to offer your next employer. Making a career move is a strategic activity. Don't do it lightly or without thoroughly investigating the companies you're considering. Where you work and whom you work for are too important and integral to your overall career experience to approach with laziness. Do your research and evaluate potential employers critically.

So how do you gauge growth opportunity with a potential employer, large or small, while still communicating your interest in the job at hand? In your next interview, ask your interviewer, *"When I'm successful in this position, and achieving all the company intends for me to achieve, what are my options for professional growth and development?"* I like this question for a couple of reasons: it assumes success for the company and for you; and it makes a statement about your desire to be with the company long-term, which despite conflicting messages, is still a good thing when it serves you too. When you ask a question like this, resist the temptation to fill in any quiet moments that follow. Just listen. Side-note: you can download a list of my current favorite interview questions to ask of your next potential employer at my website.

Chapter 6

A Note to Professional Sales Newbies

IF YOU HAVE divined that a professional sales career is in your future, honor the profession, and get yourself reputable sales training within a business-to-business selling environment (B2B). Just do it. If you didn't start as a sales professional but want to be one now, don't try to cut corners when you're told you don't have professional selling experience. Go and get it.

Inside sales isn't the same beast as outside sales, and both require different selling skills to be successful. No one should have to justify this reality to you. If you're still in high school, get your four-year college degree and find your first B2B sales role within an organization with excellent sales training. If you're in college, stay in college, then go get your first B2B sales role.

B2B sales is the foundation for professional selling in any healthcare space, dentistry included. No other type of professional experience replaces or subverts the need for professional B2B sales training and experience. I find when I say this to sales candidates, it separates the wheat from the chaff. The people who are truly cut out for a professional sales career in healthcare follow this counsel and hunt down that first sales role. Those that don't generally just never return to the conversation. Professional selling in the dental industry requires sound preparation and training, the right personal constitution for a sales career, and ongoing commitment to sharpening your selling skills. It's actually not a very long list of requirements, as lists go.

Story: Sales Rep Bootcamp

About three years ago, I had the good fortune to meet a young CFO, who we'll call John. John told his brother, a professional sales rep with a manufacturer in the dental industry, he didn't want to be a CFO anymore. What he really wanted to do was start a career in professional sales in the dental industry, and his brother pointed him to me. I'm not sure if his brother thought I'd talk him out of it or into it, but I'm grateful for the referral, either way. John emailed me to request a call, and we got one scheduled. At that point, looking at John's CFO resume, I wasn't sure what I'd be able to do to help him get where he wanted to go. But the dialog began.

John had a finance degree, accounting experience, and a handful of years working with a family-owned company in another industry as CFO. It wasn't clear to me what, if any, part of his career would translate over to the new sales career. What mattered in the end, was John's ability to take coaching. Let that sink in.

John's willingness to take coaching was the ENTIRE difference between being a CFO in another industry and being a professional sales rep in the dental industry (making less money, at first, I might add). John made this happen. Here's what I told John to do: first, go get yourself a reputable B2B sales position and kill it. Hit all your targets, track your own financial contribution to the company's bottom line (your stats), and stay in touch with me on your progress. Despite the brevity of our conversation, I was serious. Apparently, so was he. He called me when he got the B2B sales position with ADP, a company well-known for sales training. He called me when he hit his targets, and when he blew past his targets. It was so much fun to cheer for him along the way and see him accomplish his goals! Fifteen months from when he heard me tell him to get his B2B experience underway, he called me from his car to tell me he'd been recruited to sell for a manufacturer in the dental industry. Booyah!

John took coaching, didn't complain about the year it would take, and made it count. I told him he needed to get the B2B selling role because reputable B2B sales companies provide foundational sales training. That's the key. It's training you can build upon. To take your profession seriously, you need to treat it seriously, getting the training you need at the start as well as the training you need along the way, to not only win the sales role in healthcare, but to actually be outstanding at it!

No one gets into a professional sales career to be mediocre. I sure as hell didn't. And dentistry is a special place, as we've already discussed. It deserves growth-minded individuals who are dedicated to it. To be here, you need to sharpen your sword regularly. If you try to cut the B2B corner, it's a sign that professional sales may not be the career for you.

So what do you have vs what do you need? John knew where he wanted to go and where he was starting. He heard me tell him what he needed to add to his skill sets and proceeded to go and get it. He let the recruiters come to him—and they did. The fifteen months of John's life he spent employed purposefully to gain strong sales training translated directly to a financially rewarding sales career in the dental industry doing exactly what he set out to do. But really, he just followed directions.

John also had the aptitude for a professional sales career which became evident when he took the leap and got himself hired by ADP. A professional sales career in any industry is about dedication and commitment. Bravery and perseverance are required attributes for success. If one year of your professional career is too much to dedicate to the discovery of whether or not this career is truly for you, then the answer is it isn't. On the other hand, if you can get onboard with the commitment of your time to determine if a professional sales career is right for you, go get your first B2B selling role and call me in a year.

**A special note to clinical professionals who want to transition to a professional sales career in the dental industry.

There are a lot of valid reasons to desire a career in professional sales. If you're a clinician in the practice, or perhaps a treatment coordinator or another role with shared responsibility for gaining case acceptance and selling the treatment plan, you may be looking longingly at an outside sales career. We all know practicing dentistry can take its toll on your body. You may be ready to take all the clinical knowledge you've gained and put it to use somewhere less taxing on your back, your neck, and your wrists, and more profitable for your bank account. You've probably also received some light coaching and encouragement from well-meaning reps that come into your practice regularly, or some other sales professional who sees your promise. You may have heard things like, "If you can sell dentistry, you can sell anything."

So you've been dreaming about how great a sales career outside the practice will be, and I'm about to say the other thing you've probably heard at least once, but would rather not believe: selling treatment plans and gaining case acceptance is real sales, but it isn't the same type of professional selling required for a career in outside sales with a dental distributor or a manufacturer.

In point of fact, selling treatment plans and gaining case acceptance is business-to-client (B2C) sales, not business-to-business (B2B). This is the part where you want to push back because you know in your heart of hearts you will be a kick-ass sales rep. I'll bet you've seen some reps come into your practice who make you think, "If they can do it, surely I can do it." You may be right on both counts. But here are the facts you need to hear: all sales experiences are not the same; if you can sell treatment planning and gain case acceptance, that does not mean you can sell anything else; all the clinical knowledge you have doesn't outweigh the need to have professional outside sales training. In fact, if you accept that now and go get yourself into your first outside B2B sales position in another industry, I want to hear from you! I want to cheer for you when you're going after that first B2B sales role, when you're above plan and tracking toward Rookie-of-the-Year, and when you can come back to me and say, "I'm ready!" You'll be a force to be reckoned with.

If you heed this counsel, not only will I be knocking on your door in the not-too-distant future, but there will be other recruiters chasing you down and competing with me for the chance to present you to their healthcare clients. You're going to be very popular!

CHAPTER 7

PLOTTING YOUR COURSE SUCCESSFULLY

FIRST AND FOREMOST, there is no perfect company to discover and no perfect sales manager to hire under. There are only choices, and better choices. Once you dive into thinking critically about your career and all that goes into it, be excited about finding the better choices. You're in charge here, and you are able to build the future you want to have.

As you start to lay out your plan and evaluate professional sales opportunities in dental, be on the lookout for opportunities that will challenge you personally in some significant way. In a career as independent as professional sales, you've got to keep raising your own bar. Advancement in your sales career hinges on it.

So what might that look like? Challenge is a relative word, and this aspect of your search may be more introspective and geared for inward accountability. I'm speaking specifically about how we make improvements in our character and grow in emotional intelligence and self-awareness. I'm not an expert in emotional intelligence or anything like that, but a sales professional who lacks emotional intelligence is a person with limits on just how far they can take their career. Lacking self-awareness, they can be easy to spot. They don't usually take personal accountability when they're involved in conflict or a sale goes off-course. Often they're the people who will tell you their sales numbers are down because of things outside of their control—and they're down a lot. They are always working for or under a manager who is a *micromanager*, as if that's their unique misfortune.

I meet reps who see their manager as the reason for their poor performance. This person often spends a significant amount of energy in our conversation trying to tell me they'd be a top sales performer if it weren't for the micromanager who slows them down every day or keeps changing their compensation plan. This same person usually isn't open to challenging dialog with me about the lessons they may or may not be culling from the time they're spending feeling put-upon by their manager. They see taking another position, selling something else somewhere else, as their only option for growth, and they may demonstrate a pattern of changing jobs every several months or couple of years. Often, they present in interviews with a chip on their shoulder.

I can't afford to spend time with these types of reps, nor can any of my clients. These sales reps limit themselves and everyone who engages with them. Anyone who lacks emotional intelligence may have these character traits in common. But because we're in sales, we need to *get real* about this. As sales professionals, with advanced abilities to influence and direct complex selling interactions, we need to work relentlessly to be the best human beings we can be. We need to hold ourselves up to the highest ethical standards, take accountability for issues in our professional relationships, and suck the marrow from

THE CHOCOLATE ROOM

every learning event in our paths. I want to underscore that some growth experiences hurt, and the way we feel after failures can be graphic. We choose, in these cases, whether to run from them or stick around and fight virtuously to grow from the experience.

By contrast, the sales professional with emotional intelligence who chooses to learn from every complex interaction, regardless of how uncomfortable it is for them, will keep growing personally and professionally. This person will grow in character and take their career all the way to the finish line. They will likely take others along with them. This person is unstoppable. I want this sales pro in my professional network and referring their like-minded colleagues to me as well.

I spoke to a sales candidate recently who was starting to feel the discomfort and dread of going into a job every day with a senior sales manager who was being very controlling and micro-managing his work schedule even though he was above plan and not behind in completing his reports. For all intents and purposes, this sales manager ought to have been treating him like a pitcher throwing a no-hitter and left him alone! This is a candidate I would clone and build a team from: very humble top performer and a tireless hunter. He calls me and says, "I think I really need to look for a new opportunity. Every time I check my phone there's a message from him on it about something he thinks I need to do or a report he wants me to send him. He calls me on the weekends and has no boundaries at all. I love my clients, and I'm above plan, but my manager is making me hate my job." Completely logical, completely reasonable response to feeling the weight of a big thumb. Notice, he was still hitting his numbers.

We spent most of the conversation discussing the scope and size of the next sales role he wanted to find as he tracked toward his first sales management role. As a final thought on the topic, I asked him, more for confirmation than anything else, "Have you learned all you can from this experience? It will take a little while to find the right, next role. How will you keep yourself in the game in the meantime?" Silence and a groan from his side of the conversation before he says, "Dammit, I knew you were gonna' ask me that!" Pause to groan again. "If I'm moving toward sales management for myself, I can pull more out of this that'll make me a better manager in the future, and that's what I need to focus on." Yes, exactly. He knew the answer, and it wasn't comfortable for him to contemplate staying in his current role to continue working with this manager who wanted to know where he was and what he was doing at all times.

Let's be clear, micromanagers slow us down and cramp our styles. When his direct sales manager should have been taking obstacles out of his way to support his sales growth, he was making things harder than they needed to be and eating into the prime selling hours of his day. But he was actually in the perfect scenario to pay close attention to what *not* to do with the sales reps he will go on to hire in the future for his own sales team. Furthermore, learning to manage up and influence change from a less powerful position is a phenomenal skill to have, and it's rare. If he chooses to shift his perspective in order to extract all the learning from his current role and circumstances under a micromanager, he will know exactly what it looks like to micromanage someone else and be that much more prepared to recognize the personal temptations and resist them when they come up for him personally.

Side-note: Every new sales manager coming from a successful individual contributor role has to shed some layers of personal control over sales outcome. For most leaders, it isn't an easy transition to make. Making it successfully requires a real balancing act between giving your reps room to make mistakes and knowing when to be more present with them for coaching. This is an area where self-awareness goes a long way, and even the best leaders can struggle to control the temptation to micromanage their sales reps. Sometimes it can just sneak up on you (she says from personal experience). Micromanagement drives reps into the arms of other employers all the time.

Back to my candidate on the phone. He decides to grow through this time rather than bolt, and purposefully learn how to be a better sales manager for someone else in the future. It's not an indefinite amount of time that he has to keep struggling, just long enough for the right next role to come along. It may not get more comfortable working for his manager in the meantime, but purpose mitigates discomfort and leads to meaning. Learning from discomfort is a choice, and not only does it show he has emotional intelligence and self-awareness, but his character will grow in the process. Not to mention, how great will it be to be able to talk about that learning process in the next real interview he has? Answer: really, really great! It's the type of growth story from his own experience that will inspire confidence in an interviewer, and it ought to. It's also one of the reasons I like working with this particular candidate. He chooses to be coachable, and you can't keep him down. As he continues to learn about complex selling through relationships and interactions he has with his clients and leaders, he takes accountability for his own career progression. I will relish directing promising reps to his teams in the future, too. The dude's a powerhouse. Professional sales is a mighty career with significant potential for power and financial gain. Each of us is responsible to use our powers for good, and to do that we have to consistently raise our own bars.

To plot your sales career course, once you know where you're going and from what point you're beginning, choose to grow through every experience along the way. Use what you've learned about your values and the type of rep you naturally are to select sales opportunities with companies and managers that suit you and challenge you to grow in multiple ways.

Manufacturing or distribution, W2'd or independent, you will find the steps that get you to your finish line. You'll hit snags in the plan, trip over unforeseen circumstances, and need to recalibrate, maybe multiple times. The best of us do. But with every challenge you surmount and every lesson you suck in, you're growing up, personally and professionally. When you veer off course, you won't stall out or lose your way entirely. You'll keep getting up. Remember, in a professional sales career, perseverance and bravery are required.

Chapter 8

What the Dental Industry Still Needs

FOR ALL DENTAL has to offer to sales professionals, it's light in a few critical areas necessary for it to continue to thrive in an advanced US economy: professional networking activities, skillful interviewing technique, and new professional sales talent (aka you).

There are networking events that happen regularly in the dental industry at dental shows and throughout the year for legacy companies, professional clinicians, and dental practices both independent and corporate. We all have access to social media, and everyone knows how to find someone who's like them, *blah, blah, blah.*

None of these existing networking platforms meets the needs of the dental industry to connect the older manufacturers and distributors to new ones and bring together people of varied backgrounds and experiences. There isn't currently an option for all start-ups to get together with the legacy companies, or even with each other for that matter, or for brand new company pioneers to learn from industry veterans. There is no existing channel for passing down the history of the industry without losing valuable knowledge and information from the trade side. Ironically, oral tradition breaks down at this point. In the only established trade-side organization that I know of where the companies in dentistry come together *without* clients around, the price of entry is too high for most start-ups in their first crucial years of business to engage; they're priced-out.

This lonely trade organization is a closed system and is quickly nearing its expiration date. Once that date arrives, the trade side of the industry will be left with only dental shows to drive interaction. If you sell for a distributor, your company's annual sales meeting will draw manufacturing partners. But if you work for a company that doesn't sell through distribution, you won't be invited to interact at that level either. Incidentally, many of the legacy dental distributors in the country belong to this expiring trade organization. Once these distribution companies stop coming together to gain exposure to diverse new manufacturers entering the market, a crucial professional aspect of industry relationships and community will fall to the wayside and be lost.

So what? Why should anyone care?

When community breaks down in any civilization, uniting values erode, and in this case, professionalism is one of those values. For the dental industry to continue to stand out among healthcare industries where you might want to plant your sales career, a place where growth-focused professionals, pioneers, and independence thrive, we need a more fruitful way to recycle knowledge, information, and values. We need a new trade association, and we need it to bring together start-ups and legacy companies in both distribution and manufacturing, without the customer around.

New blood refreshes innovation and raises the bar for the business of oral care. Getting together without clinicians around lowers barriers to partnership and takes the edge off. It makes for an environment where the trade side of dental can benefit from knowledge-sharing from multiple backyards.

Furthermore, it's important to continue to revive traditions that guard the professionalism of the industry. The dental trade, particularly the distribution side of it, is the protector of the clinician's autonomy, and at times, even their integrity. Independent dental distributors know our clinicians best, guard their independence best, and remind us of times when every sale happened face-to-face and handshake-to-handshake.

Getting together as a trade also protects distribution. You don't have to sell through distribution to see its relevance to the industry. We need the distribution stories to be passed down versus die off. There is a symbiotic relationship in dentistry consisting of trade and clinical influences. It isn't enough to nurture just one side and forget the other. To ensure the health of the dental community as a whole, we need an alumni organization for the trade. It's an abundance philosophy.

Interviewing Etiquette

Every sales professional who wants to find an open door to the Chocolate Room, aka the dental industry, should revisit the lessons of business professionalism that were taught to young adults in the previous century—basic interview etiquette:

Dress to impress;

Greet your interviewer with a firm handshake;

Keep reasonable eye contact;

Bring at least three fresh copies of your resume to every in-person interview;

Follow up your interview with a professionally written note of gratitude, regardless of whether or not the interviewer has chosen to move you forward in the interview process;

Over-prepare for every interview you have;

Verbal acceptance of an offer of employment is a real commitment.

Regardless of whether or not anyone ever told you these behaviors were necessary or expected, you won't escape the consequences for neglecting them. Disregard, and kiss your new sales opportunity goodbye. It doesn't matter how many months or years of professional sales experience you bring to the table if you don't conduct yourself like a professional once you're there. By the same token, the trade side of the industry needs a refresher on Interviewing 101:

Be on time to your interviews and don't keep a candidate waiting;

Carve out a proper amount of time in your day/ schedule for the interview plus thirty minutes;

Don't take calls or allow interruptions during your interview, because your candidate's time is as important as your own while you're together;

Prepare for your interview by dedicating time to read the candidate's resume, and plan questions around their experience in advance;

Listen to their answers attentively and take notes;

Hold your interviews in public places that are well-lit and free from distractions;

Show your candidates respect and follow up with feedback at an established and agreed-upon time;

A verbal offer of employment is a commitment, but your candidate should have it in writing within the hour.

It is a marriage, after all. Dating, courting, proposal of marriage. Prospecting, interviewing, accepting the offer to marry. Some might argue there's still a chance to change your mind between proposal and marriage. Not only do I disagree with that assertion, I find it evidence of low moral character. Be prepared, assess your options critically, and live like your word is of great worth because, in fact, it is.

Once you offer employment, as a company, and accept employment, as a candidate, whether verbally or in writing, the deal is done. Backing out constitutes breach of contract in either direction, and I'm serious as a heart attack. While I always tell candidates to get it in writing, a company who makes a verbal offer is committed as soon as the words hit the air, and backing out of the offer made is particularly egregious and unforgivable. Don't burn bridges with dishonesty or empty commitment language, and don't burn your recruiter. It's time to revive professionalism.

All that's left now is you.

Professional selling skills and experience...check! Clear goals and values...check-check! Industry research done...check!

The dental industry needs you. Trail blazers, pioneers, risk-takers, geniuses, brave souls, and people of purpose, bring your professional selling skills to the dental industry and make your mark.

You've been told, I'm sure, you need to "get out there and network," and, "it's about who you know." Both are true, but not complete on their own. In fact, just about anything you would do to secure a new client in your territory, you should be thinking about doing to secure your next professional sales opportunity in dental. Networking is about introducing yourself to new individuals while bringing them value.

Every time you ever went out cold-calling, you were networking. You know how to do this, and as a sales professional it should be second nature. Think of your career hunt as the most important cold-calling you need to be doing on a regular basis, and employ your own resourcefulness to win the sale. Don't let rejection be the blow that keeps you down. Get up again every time. Do your research and investigate your options. Generate your outcome with solid preparation and critical thinking. Follow up. Show gratitude. Give of yourself generously, but not wastefully. Do what you say you'll do. Be intentional and purposeful. Plant yourself where you can grow and become an integral part of something bigger than you. The dental industry will get even cooler with you in it. You've got this, and I'm cheering for you.

Conclusion

IT'S YOUR TURN now. Do you have what it takes? Will you come in? I'd love it if you'd share your resume with me at my website. I'll want to know where I can find you when clients ask me for professional sales talent with brains, heart, and stamina. I wonder where our next conversation will go. Which direction you'll be most interested in heading. I wonder whom you'll bring with you. I hope to see you at the zoo, investigating your options. The conversation has already begun, and it's a good one. I wonder what you'll teach us when you get here. I wonder how you'll connect with the dental community and be part of the horsepower under the hood. I wonder what you'll do with everything that awaits you.

There you have it. I've played the musical lock for you. The door to the dental industry is open. Enter here.

GLOSSARY

Hunter: type of sales rep who has a consistent and unflagging desire to prospect for new business.

Account Manager: type of sales rep who is more focused on retaining existing business than on prospecting for new business relationships.

Associate sales rep: a category of sales role involving significant training in preparation for promotion to a full territory sales rep.

SAM/NAM: terms used to denote strategic account management or national account management; these titles accompany more senior selling roles that are specialized, or which cater to larger or significant account clients.

Prospecting/hunting: locating and calling on new accounts where no previous selling relationship has been established (see also cold calling).

B2B: business to business sale where both the seller is a business entity and the buyer is a business entity who will use the product purchased in the service of their clients.

B2C: business to client sale where the seller is a business entity and the buyer is the end user of the product.

Riffed: laid off; terminated from employment as part of an overall reduction of workforce versus *for cause* which may involve lack of positive performance.

Rookie: brand new salesperson, usually in their first full year of selling professionally for a specific company.

Carrying a bag: selling a product in the field to a customer

Outside sales/In the field: face to face selling, not to be confused with sales over the phone, or inside sales.

Inside Sales: sales conducted over the telephone.

At the C-Suite/C-level: executive levels of a corporation including VP level and above.

Sales cycle: the period of time it usually takes to sell a particular type of product. A sales cycle usually varies based on product type and frequency of purchase.

Long sales cycle: term that describes a period of time greater than a year during which a product is sold to a buyer. Capital sales traditionally employ longer sales cycles than consumable sales.

Short sales cycle: term that describes a period of time less than a year during which a product is sold to a buyer. Consumable sales traditionally employ shorter sales cycles than capital equipment sales.

Med device: medical device is a category of sale where the product is placed within the boundaries of the human body during some type of surgical procedure. These products require FDA approval for use in patients.

Consumable: category of sale where the product is sold and needs to be resold to the buyer on a regular basis. An example of a consumable product is toothpaste.

Capital equipment: category of sale where the product is purchased by the buyer only once in a significant period of time; product is also usually more expensive, and the sales cycle is longer than with a consumable product. An example of a capital sale is a dental chair.

Small equipment: category of sale where the product may be purchased in quantity greater than one and usually is less expensive than a capital sale, but not considered a consumable sale. An example of a small equipment sale is a handpiece. Handpieces are usually purchased one to an operatory.

Operatory: term used to refer to the area in a practice where a patient receives dental treatment. An operatory contains a dental chair, cabinetry, lighting, and other small equipment used in standard dental procedures.

Technology sale: term used to refer to any type of sale in the dental practice involving a product that needs to have operating software updated regularly in order to operate successfully. Examples of technology sales are practice management software and digital imaging equipment.

Digital Imaging: term referring to any aspect of image capture that does not include the use of film but is instead captured digitally with sensors and/or software.

CAD-CAM: computer-aided design: computer-aided manufacturing

Cold-calling: contact made by a sales rep to a potential client without any prior buying relationship established first.

Ride-along: the term used to describe accompanying the sales rep in visiting customers during the course of a business day.

Lunch-n-learn: term used to describe the activity of presenting product training or detailing during a break in the day, and usually over lunch in the practice.

Distributor: mid-point supplier of products and services who represents multiple brands and product line choices.

Manufacturer: maker of the product

Sales through distribution: method of selling where the product manufacturer partners with a mid-point supplier in order to get the manufactured product sold into a larger swath of clients than can be reached in a one-to-one ratio.

Direct sales: method of selling that involves no mid-point supplier but utilizes a one-to-one ratio of sales rep to client.

Sales manager: leader over a team of sales reps who has direct financial accountability for the activities of the team. This person can hire and fire employees.

W2'd: employed by a company and not an independent contractor

1099: independent contractor and not employed by a company

DDS: Doctor of Dental Surgery

DMD: Doctor of Medicine in Dentistry

Associate dentist: the dentist in the practice who is not the owner of the practice.

RDH: Registered Dental Hygienist

CDA: Certified Dental Assistant

Caries: the official word for cavities

Intraoral: inside the mouth cavity

KOL/key opinion leader: a professional who carries significant influence among their peers and affects buying decisions.

Preventive: term in dentistry meant to denote services or procedures that prevent the spread of caries or tooth decay and protect dentin.

Restorative: term in dentistry that denotes services or procedures that repair dentin or entirely replace teeth to restore the smile.

About the Author

PAIGE MEAD has been recruiting professionally for over twenty years. She opens doors and connects people for a living in the dental industry. As an industry ambassador and key opinion leader, her role is to draw in and hold onto the professional sales and executive talent that will drive the industry for the next century. Paige Mead Recruiting is a niche recruiting firm specializing in sales and executive search for the dental industry.